D0438368

the year of goodbyes

the year of goodbyes

A true story of friendship, family, and farewells

DEBBIE LEVY

Disney • Hyperion Books
New York

For my mother, Jutta Salzberg Levy

Copyright © 2010 by Debbie Levy

Printed in the United States of America

First Edition

1 3 5 7 9 10 8 6 4 2

V567-9638-5-10001

This book is set in 13-point Cochin
Reinforced binding

Library of Congress Cataloging-in-Publication Data on file.

ISBN 978-1-4231-2901-1

Visit www.hyperionbooksforchildren.com

Introduction

✶

This book is based on another book—not a library book, or a bookstore book, or even a typed manuscript. It was a book written by hand and owned by my mother when she lived in Germany as a girl. The year was 1938. In her own language, German, the book was known as a *poesiealbum* (po-eh-ZEE ALbum). In English, you could call it a poetry album.

Poesiealbums were blank books in which young people—mostly girls—collected poems, drawings, and expressions of good wishes from friends and family. The books were popular in Germany in the 1930s, and had been fashionable since the 1800s. The closest American traditions were autograph books and school yearbooks—but *poesiealbums* were much more serious enterprises. You didn't just dash off a little ditty while leaning against a locker in the school hallway. Usually you took your friend's *poesiealbum* home overnight and used your best handwriting, and maybe also colored pencils, to create a lasting impression. Your illustrations were likely to include symbols of good luck, such as ladybugs, piles of coins, horseshoes, fly mushrooms, four-leaf clovers, hearts, and chimney sweeps and their tools. You might further decorate your page with *oblaten* (o-BLAH-ten), stickers that girls collected and traded.

In 1938, World War II had not yet begun, but Germany, under its leader Adolf Hitler and the Nazi Party, had certainly begun its policies of discrimination and exclusion toward the nation's Jews. My mother, her family, and most of her friends were Jewish. The entries in my mother's *poesiealbum*, written from January to November of 1938, were made during a period of rapidly increasing danger for Jews in Germany.

This book—the book you have in your hands—tells the story of what happened to my mother and her family in 1938. The actual *poesiealbum* entries by my mother's friends and family (translated here into English) serve as stepping stones through the months of this crucial year. They introduce chapters, written in verse form, that describe my mother's experiences and emotions and report some of the history of the era. I have written these verses in consultation with my mother to reflect her voice, feelings, and thoughts as she was living through this memorable year. Finally, the book also includes excerpts from my mother's diary, which she began in the fall of 1938. Together the *poesie* writings, verses, and diary entries reflect a year of change and chance, confusion and cruelty. Perhaps most of all, they describe a year of goodbyes.

I

Don't Make a Mess

January 1938

Jutta Salzberg
Sauberkeit ist eine Zier
jeden Fleck verbiet ich
mir

Behold my album's cleanliness,
*and when you write don't make a mess.**

*Translated literally, the words mean, "Cleanliness is a virtue/Please don't leave any spots." But in German, the words at the ends of the two lines rhyme—*Zier* and *mir*. So the quip is actually more playful than an exact translation suggests, more like "Behold my album's cleanliness,/and when you write don't make a mess." Translating rhyming poetry is often a matter of interpretation like this. To capture the overall sense or feeling of the poem, the translator must sometimes go beyond a simple word-by-word translation. This is the approach taken in this book.

I write these words
on the very first page
of my brand-new book,
my wordless,
untouched,
blank-new book
with sturdy brown covers,
like heels of bread
spread with smooth butter pages inside —
my favorite sandwich.
It's what we all write
(in German)
at the front of our books,
our empty, inviting
poesie books,
before we ask friends
to fill up the pages
with poems and promises,
wishes and warnings,
names and dates.

It is January 1938.
I am Jutta* Salzberg,
a Jewish girl
in the city of Hamburg,
between the Elbe and Alster rivers,
in the north of Germany.

*Jutta is pronounced YU-tah.

II

What Is Will?
Monday, January 24, 1938

> *Wille ist Macht*
>
> *Zur Erinnerung*
> *an deiner frühren*
> *Mittschülerin*
>
> *Lisa Streit*
>
> d.24.I.38

Will is power.

To remember your former classmate,
Lisa Streit
January 24, 1938

How serious this sounds,
how unlike Lisa,
who is full of fun.
The fun's still there,
but the serious takes up more space,
and so Lisa gets right to the point,
which is:
We are Jews in Germany,
in Hitler's Nazi Germany,
and the Nazis hate Jews
with a power so strong
we must match their hate
with *will*.

What is will?
It's courage. It's strength.
It's seeing the Nazi hate everywhere —
signs in restaurants that say
JEWS UNWELCOME,
signs in stores,
JUDEN VERBOTEN,
no Jews on playgrounds,
no Jews in libraries. . . .
It's feeling the Nazi hate
and laughing with your girlfriends anyway.

No Jews as Germans. Yes, this is a law!
And this is truly something
to laugh at.
Lisa's family has been German forever —

generations of Jewish Germans,
speaking German,
playing German music,
reading German books.
Lisa's family is more German than Adolf Hitler!
(He comes from Austria.)
But now — *poof!* — they are not German.
Now — *abracadabra!* — Jews are not Germans.
It is the law.
Jews are only Jews
and "pure" Germans are Aryans,
which is the special name
the Nazis made up for themselves.

Speaking of names,
here is another law:
No Jews with names that sound Aryan.
Like what — Adolf?

Will is power, Lisa writes.
Sometimes *will* is laughing at crazy rules
(quietly, privately,
for we wouldn't want the Nazis to hear).
But sometimes —
will is tickets to leave Germany.
That's what Lisa and her family have:
tickets for a big ship
to take them to America.
They leave in a few weeks.

Will is power.
But for me,
it is hard to have will.
It is hard to feel power
when a friend is leaving.

III

With Hands That Are Ever Filled
Tuesday, January 25, 1938

May joy and pleasure be yours
throughout your long-lived days,
with hands that are ever filled
with luck and blessings always.

With thoughts from your classmate,
Ilse Hess
Hamburg, January 25, 1937

I think my friend Ilse
was working so hard
to write her *poesie*
in her fanciest formal script
that she forgot what year it is.
It's a mistake many of us make
in January,
even when writing
in ordinary script.
After twelve months
of writing *1937*,
the habit is not yet broken.

Or maybe it's wishful thinking.
Maybe Ilse wishes
she could flip the calendar
backward to January 1937.
One year ago,
there was Hitler,
there were Nazis,
there was hate,
but it was softer,
quieter.
Father says
it was because of
the Olympic Games,
held in Berlin in 1936.
With the world watching,
the Nazis behaved,
for a while.

I wish I could turn back time, too.
Not only because the hate was softer,
but also because my very favorite uncle,
Uncle Max, was still here,
with his wife, Aunt Alice.
I loved to sleep over
at their apartment.
They have no children,
but they love children,
me in particular.
At night
in their apartment,
we drank cups of tea
with sugar cubes
and ate pieces of *linzertorte*.
Before bed
we put sugar cubes
on the windowsill—
for the stork, we said.

The stork never came.
Uncle Max and Aunt Alice
have sailed to America.
Maybe there, the stork will find them.
Maybe there, their hands will be filled
with the baby they crave,
with luck and blessings,
with the softness and quiet
of a different year
in a different place.

IV

Thinking of God
Wednesday, January 26, 1938

> Mit G"tt fang an,
> Mit G"tt hör auf,
> das ist der beste Lebenslauf.
>
> Dies wünscht Dir
> Deine
> Freundin
> Inge Weiss.
>
> Den 26.1.38

Let God be the beginning.
Let God be the end.
This is the best course in life.

This is what I wish for you, my friend.
Inge Weiss
January 26, 1938

Inge writes of God,
but she is not very religious.
I am not very religious, either,
nor are most of my friends.
Some more than others —
like Ruth Carlebach,
whose father is the most important rabbi
here in Hamburg.

Everyone knows Rabbi Joseph Carlebach.
Everyone knows he knows
everything about God and Torah,
and other things besides.
Does he know
about Ruth's little tastes of *trayfe**
at her friends' houses,
tiny slivers of ham
just to see what it's like?
I bet he does.
Ruth is curious; can you blame her?
I bet he doesn't.
I bet he knows
that girls aren't always perfect,
not even daughters of rabbis.

My family goes to synagogue
for the big holidays,
but not much otherwise.

*Trayfe refers to forbidden, or nonkosher, foods, including ham and other pork products.

We used to have big Passover seders,
with lots of friends and food.
We didn't keep kosher even before
the Nazis outlawed kosher meat.

Imagine all the delicious treats
from the wonderful German delicatessen
I would have missed if we were kosher!
(Oh, the bologna! Oh, the ham —
yes, ham.
I am one of Ruth Carlebach's tempters.)
We don't go to that deli anymore.
They don't want us as customers.
JEWS NOT DESIRED, the sign says.

Whether we are religious
or not religious,
all of my friends and I attend
the Jewish School for Girls.
Why?
Simple:
We are all Jews,
and the Germans don't want us
in their schools.
For me it started when a nice lady
at my old school —
my public school,
where non-Jews and Jews learned together —
called me out of class
for something she called "race research."

I was seven years old.
She asked me many questions
about my family,
about my "racial characteristics."
I didn't know I had any.
But the Nazis say Jews are
a separate race,
a bad and dirty race,
an alien race.
So the nice lady's questions
were not really nice at all.
That was the end
of city schools for me.
Mother and Father took me out.

And after a while,
the Nazis said Jews could not attend the city schools,
even if they didn't mind being treated badly
and being called dirty Jew
by teachers and other kids.

So now we are all Jews,
together in our all-Jewish private school.
I suppose this makes us feel
more Jewish than we did before,
even those among us who felt
more German than Jewish.
I suppose this also makes us think
about God
more than we used to.

Inge has never spoken to me
of God before.
But then, many things are happening,
and many things are being spoken of,
that never happened
and were never spoken of
before.

V

Honor
Wednesday, January 26, 1938

Die alten ehre stest
Du bleibst nicht ewig Kind
Sie waren was Du bist
Und Du wirst was sie
sind.

Dieses Schrieb Dir Deine
Freundin

Cilly Seligmann

Bern 26.1.38.

Always honor your elders;
you will not be a child forever.
They were once as you are,
and you will be what they are now.

Written for you by your friend,
Cilly Seligmann
January 26, 1938

Always, Cilly? *Always?*
I should honor the Walls,
my parents' friends,
even after Herr Wall
stopped playing cards with Father?
Even after they stopped
going on beach vacations with us,
to the North Sea,
because we are Jewish
and they are not?

Always, Cilly?
When I still went to the German school,
one day my class
went on a big trip downtown
to hear an important man speak.
There he was,
up on a platform,
above the crowd.
Only he wasn't speaking,
he was screaming.
He was screaming,
and we had to salute him,
because he was Hitler,
the Führer,
the leader.
On the radio, too,
I hear him screaming.
He tells big lies about Jews,
then talks about German "honor."

Always honor your elders.
They were once as you are.

Hitler is my elder.
Was he once as I am?
I can't believe that.
Will I become what he is now?
I know I will not.
And anyway, imagine
what he would say about it,
about a Jew being, or becoming,
like him.

Always honor your elders.
It's a fine idea, but
always
is a very long time;
as for *honor* —
it can be hard to know what that means.

VI

Near and Far
Monday, February 7, 1938

Willst Du in die Ferne schweifen?
Sieh, das Gute liegt so nah.
Lerne nur das Glück ergreifen,
Und das Glück ist immer da!

Dies l. Jutta schrieb
Dir Deine Schulkameradin
Ruth Sperber.

Abg. d. 7.2.38.

Do you wish to roam so far?
Look, the good is near.
Just learn to seize luck,
And luck will always be here. *

This, dear Jutta, was written for you
by your schoolmate, Ruth Sperber
February 7, 1938

*This poem is by the German writer Johann Wolfgang von Goethe, who lived from 1749 to 1832.

19

I *do* want to roam,
no matter what Ruth writes.
I miss my old life —
streetcar rides downtown
just for fun,
outings in Father's automobile,
roller-skating around the neighborhood,
games of tag in the street,
fairs in the Stadtpark
in the center of Hamburg,
when they brought in
the carousel,
a puppet show,
little donkeys to ride —
how fun for everyone!
Parades, festivals, Christmas markets!
I loved them all.

Until last autumn.
It was a festival day,
a German holiday.
Dusk was falling.
We were walking with our neighbors,
my friends and I,
safely (we thought) in our neighborhood,
holding paper lanterns
like all German kids do on this day,
lighting up the darkening street
with our parade of flickering candles,
singing the song all German kids know:

Lantern, lantern,
Sun, moon, and stars,
we sang,
Burn on, my light,
Burn on, my light,
But not my dear lantern —
and those German boys,
proud in their Hitler Youth uniforms,
threw rocks at us
and pushed us off the sidewalk.
"Jewish race polluters!"

Now I am not allowed
to go about as I please.
I cannot even play outside
as I used to, as I want to,
because there is no such thing anymore as
safely in our neighborhood.

So then,
I want to say to Ruth Sperber,
if here in my own neighborhood
there are children who will
throw stones at me,
spit on me,
yell at me,
then the good is *not* so near,
is it?

And if the good is not near,
why should I not roam far?

But I don't say this to my friend,
who, after all,
was only reciting a poem.

VII

Speaking of Angels
Sunday, March 27, 1938

*May three angels be with you
through all of your life,
and the angels I mean
are love, luck, and happiness.*

*To remember,
Eva Rosenbaum
March 27, 1938*

Who believes in angels?
Not me,
not Eva,
not really.
But maybe we should,
for we need them
to take us out of Germany.
That is what everyone talks about —
leaving Germany.
Going to America,
Holland, Belgium, Switzerland,
Argentina, Africa — even China!

Father used to say,
Things will get better.
He doesn't say that anymore.
Last month, the Nazis said
all Jews from Russia
must leave Germany.
This month, the Nazis marched
into Austria,
and now it's part of Germany.

Father and Mother talk
about what is happening
to Jews in Austria —
Nazis looting their belongings,
putting Jews in jail,
sending some away to Dachau,
a "concentration camp" in the south of Germany.

(I don't really know what a concentration camp is,
but I do know it's not a place you'd want to go.)

For fun, the Nazis in Austria force old Jews —
Jews who are grandmothers and grandfathers —
to scrub streets and windows
while crowds of people watch and laugh.

What next?
my parents wonder.

Lying on the couch
in our beautiful living room,
I put a feather pillow over my head
so I don't hear the answer,
and I think of Eva's angels.
First, the angel of love —
but I can't help hearing
what Father is saying.
Today he got a letter
from his brother in Detroit.
Father asked him to help us
come to America,
and his brother said,
"Yes! Come to America!
Come to Detroit and I will help you!
Like I am helping Uncle Max and Aunt Alice.
But leave your wife and children behind.
You can send for them later,
once you have earned money to pay for them.

I can't help everyone at once, after all."
"Never!" my father says.
"Never will I leave you, Rose!
Never will I leave the girls behind.
Our home, yes.
Our car, yes.
But not my family.
Not for one day."

I squeeze the pillow tighter around my ears.
I try to think about the angel of luck,
because I have learned how much luck
it will take for us to leave Germany.
I never knew how hard it was,
how you need permission
from so many people.
Permission from your relatives in America,
who must send a special letter,
called an affidavit,
promising the American officials
that they have enough money
to take care of you
if you can't take care of yourself.
Permission from American officials,
who must agree to give you an immigrant visa,
a special invitation to live in their country.
Permission from German officials,
who should be happy to give it,
since we know they don't want us here.

To get so many permissions,
plus tickets for a train or a ship or both,
it seems only an angel of luck
can make it happen —
an angel, plus Father's constant letter-writing
and planning and worrying.
Tomorrow he will write to another
relative in America,
a relative he hopes won't tell him
to leave us behind.

I am not even sure
I want us to get so lucky.
I can't play in the street anymore,
but I can still go to
the Bar Kochba Gymnastics Club —
how my vault is improving!
And I love my home,
with this couch in the living room,
where I can hear, or not hear, my parents;
with its big kitchen and, next to it,
a pantry with a window,
where I have sat so many times,
eating bread with butter,
slice after slice,
looking out at my street,
at the people walking by,
my friends,
and now, too, the German boys
in their proud brown uniforms.

What do I care about
those Hitler Youth boys
when I can still see movies?
The Waterloo Theatre doesn't care
if you're Jewish,
so I see every movie they show.

But it is not up to me
whether we get lucky or not,
whether we stay here or leave our home.
So I think about Eva's third angel,
the angel of happiness.
I hope that she —
is an angel a she or a he? —
will find me,
wherever I end up.

VIII

Parents
April 1938

Mach' dem Vater keine Sorgen
Mach' der Mutter keine Schmerz
Denn Du weißt ja nicht ob
Morgen
Dir entschläft solch treues
Herz.
Deine Schulfreundin
Rebekka Hermannsen
Hbg. d. 4. 38.

Do not cause your father any worries,
do not cause your mother any pain,
for you do not know if tomorrow
such dear hearts will pass away.

Your schoolmate,
Rebekka Hermannsen
Hamburg, April 1938

My father
is Isaac Salzberg.
My mother
is Rose Kleinert Salzberg.
Both from Poland,
they moved to Hamburg
to raise their family,
me and my little sister, Ruth.

Mother, my *Mutti*,
is a *hausfrau*, a housewife,
in charge of Ruth and me
and the apartment
and our housekeeper, Frau Krug
(with her stained teeth
and stale breath
and veal roast that everyone loves,
except me).
Mother plays the piano every day,
waves of music
washing through our home.

Father is a merchant,
who sells belts, suspenders, and garters —
things to hold other things up,
like trousers, socks, and stockings.

He is my *Vati* —
that's what I call him —
and I am his *Juttalein*.

He used to take me,
just me,
downtown to the Four Seasons Hotel
for my favorite treat:
a napoleon,
with endless layers of pastry
and whipped cream filling,
papery and silky all at once,
too indescribably delicious for words,
even for poetry words.
We sat by the window
looking at the Alster Lake
and the passersby.
I held on to every bite
for as long as I could,
and imagined the lives
of the strangers outside
as *Vati* drank his coffee
and listened to my stories.

But no longer.
I should have said
Father *was* a merchant,
who used to have an office downtown,
until he was no longer allowed to.
Then he had his office at home,
until last year, when the German factory
that makes the belts and suspenders and garters
dismissed him,
even though he is an excellent salesman,

because the Nazis don't want Jews
working as salesmen for German companies
or as bankers, stockbrokers, lawyers,
actors, professors,
or pretty much anything.

My father still works,
but his job is different now.
He is not selling goods.
He is not earning money.
His job now is to find a way
to get us out of Germany.
When I look at Father's face
at the end of the day,
I see his new job is so much harder
than his old one.
He sags,
and I think how Father could use something
to hold him up—
a belt,
a suspender,
a garter. . . .

I am glad for Mother's music,
the waltzes and preludes
on which my father can float
away from the worries and pain
at least for a little while
every day.

IX

Slipping Away
Wednesday, June 29, 1938

"Oh,, nützet der Jugendfrohe
Stunden, Sie wissen nichts von
Wiederkehr, Einmal entschlüpft,
einmal entschwunden
Zurück kehrt keine Jugend mehr.

Dies l. Jutta schrieb Dir
zum Andenken Deine
Schulkameradin
Ellen Davidsohn.

Hbg. d. 29.6.38.

Oh, take advantage of the happy hours of youth.
They will not return.
Once slipped away,
once disappeared,
youth will never return.

This, dear Jutta, I wrote for you,
with thoughts from your schoolmate,
Ellen Davidsohn
June 29, 1938

Eleven and twelve,
that's how old we are.
I can't imagine
being as old as
Mother and Father,
but I also can't imagine
not becoming as old as them.

Yes, I am eleven-and-three-quarters years old.
I used to worry about my grades
and having to eat stuffed cabbage.
I used to wonder about being invited to parties.
But now I wonder,
what will become of us?
What will become of me?

I hear my parents
and their friends
speaking of news
from Berlin and Frankfurt,
and other German cities,
where things are worse
than here in Hamburg.

In those places,
Jews are arrested
in the middle of the night,
taken from their soft beds
to the police station.

In the dark of a movie theater —
a movie theater,
one of my favorite places! —
suddenly on come the lights,
and all Jews are rounded up.
At a café, over dinner,
on a lovely summer night,
in crash the police,
and out go the Jews.

They are sent to Buchenwald,
another of the Nazis' concentration camps,
which, I have learned,
are not camps at all,
but prisons for people
who have committed no crimes.

The news comes
from shortwave radios
that my parents and their friends
listen to every day.
Broadcasts from other countries,
with foreign reporters telling
what is happening to Jews here.
Listening to these reports
is against Nazi law.
German radio stations
don't have bad news about Nazis,
only news about how bad
Jews are.

In bed at night,
with my sister, Ruthie,
breathing lightly
across the room,
I close my eyes
and see the Gestapo —
the Nazi secret police —
bursting into our home
to take us all to Buchenwald.

But when we get there,
and the Gestapo realize
that my parents really have committed a crime,
the crime of listening to shortwave radio,
they get very angry
and send us to an even worse place.

Then I open my eyes,
because I have reached the limit
of my imagination.
I can't imagine what might happen.
I can't imagine what will become of us.
I can't imagine being as old as Mother and Father.
I can't imagine not becoming as old as them.

X

Try, Try Again
Thursday, September 22, 1938

Greif an ein Werk
Und wirf den Mut
nicht bald zur Erden;
Was schwer ist,
Kann durch Fleiß und
Übung leichter werden.
Deine Mitschülerin
Ilse Behrend

Ben 22. 9. 38

Tackle your work,
and do not lose heart.
Through diligence and practice
you will master what you start.

Your classmate,
Ilse Behrend
September 22, 1938

Run, run, run
toward the vault,
jump on the springboard,
fly over,
land on my feet.
Two times each week
at the Bar Kochba club,
I diligently practice gymnastics.

Mother plays and plays
her piano,
music pouring
like *himbeere wasser* —
raspberry water —
practicing, practicing,
fragrant, flawless.

Father talks and talks
to the American officials here in Hamburg
who are in charge of the immigrant visas,
and who decide who gets to go to America,
his words dripping
like tears —
pleading, pleading.

In the summer we had good news:
Our uncle Isaac Gotthelf, who lives
in a place called Paterson, New Jersey,
sent the affidavit to the American officials
in Hamburg,

promising that he will be responsible for us —
all of us! not just Father —
if we need help in America.

And bad news:
So many Jews in Germany and Austria
want to go to America,
but America does not want us all,
and neither do other countries.

In July those countries had a big meeting,
where they decided to do exactly
nothing
about this problem.

We are lucky
because we have the affidavit from our uncle.
Some Jews in Germany
have no New Jersey uncles.
Some Jews in Berlin, we hear,
are scouring American telephone books,
hoping to find someone with their last name,
who might promise the American officials
that they will take care of their German relatives,
just please let them come to America —
like our uncle Isaac Gotthelf has promised for us.

And we are lucky
because the Nazis have given Father
our exit papers.

Yes, they say, we may leave,
just so long as we don't take with us
the money Father has earned and saved
from his years in business,
or anything valuable that we own.
This does not surprise my father.
He explains that the Nazis
are taking money and property from Jews
whether they stay in Germany or leave.
I am sickened to hear this,
sickened to hear that in America
our life will be so different,
so less nice than it has been here.

Well, nice if you forget about the Nazis.

But we are not leaving yet,
for despite all of Father's talking,
despite his diligence,
despite the affidavit,
despite the German exit papers—
we still have no visas from the Americans.

Diligence. Practice.
They are good for gymnastics.
They are good for piano.
But, I'm afraid,
they are not good
for everything.

XI

Another Book to Love
Wednesday, September 28, 1938

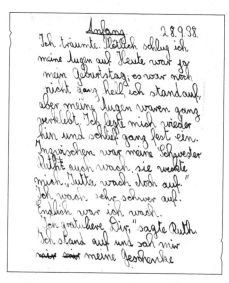

Beginning

I was dreaming. Suddenly I opened my eyes and today is my birthday. It was not yet daylight, and I got up from my bed. But I was still sleepy-eyed. I lay down again and fell fast asleep. In the meantime my sister, Ruth, woke up. She woke me: "Jutta, wake up." I awoke with difficulty. Finally I was awake. Ruth said: "Happy Birthday." I stood up and I saw my presents. Oh, how many! I got a red-and-blue pullover, four pairs of kneesocks, two pairs of pants, stockings and a garter belt, handkerchiefs, a nightgown, two pairs of pajamas, and this diary.

And from my girlfriends: from Ilse Stern, a bracelet; from Felicitas Mehl, stationery; Ilse Hess, a tricolor pen; from Ellen Davidsohn, a book; from Ruth Sperber, a book; Eva Rosenbaum, a jewelry box; from Ellen Riesenfeld, a book; Inge Weiss, a book; and from Herr Baum, stationery.

At four o'clock all the kids were to come. They all came. We sat very cozily and drank coffee and ate whipped cream tart. Then we played. Meanwhile Ruth Sperber and Inge Weiss got into a fight, and Inge Weiss was very fresh to Mother. So went the afternoon, very happily.

—diary entry for September 28, 1938

There are many worries, but
there are still birthdays —
my twelfth birthday!

There are still friends!
Some have left us —
Anita and Lisa and Irene.
We don't hear from them,
but we hope they are happy
in their new homes.
We try not to think of other girls
who have disappeared and gone —
we don't know where.

There are still presents!
My new diary is my favorite.
Now I have two books I love —
my *poesiealbum,* warm and brown,
full of friends;
and my diary,
with red covers and a snap lock,
empty, private, waiting for secrets.

XII

Whispers
Monday, October 3, 1938

Rede wenig, aber wahr
vieles Reden bringt
Gefahr!
Zum Andenken
an Deine Mitschülerin
Hannelore
Ascher

Den 2.10.38

Speak little but speak the truth.
Too much talk is dangerous!

With thoughts from your classmate,
Hannelore Ascher
October 3, 1938

Whispers, whispers.
People are whispering
because Jews are disappearing,
not just from Berlin and Frankfurt
and places far away,
but from Hamburg,
even our own neighborhood.

Especially *Ostjuden* —
eastern Jews,
those who were born
in countries to the east.
Father and Mother
were born in Poland.
Poland is to the east.
My parents are *Ostjuden*.
When will they disappear?

Hannelore and I,
and our other friends,
whisper during recess
in the backyard of our school.
Talk is dangerous, we are told.
Silence is safer.
But to me —
talk is comforting.
Silence is scary.
Things are upside down
when we have to whisper outside.

Quiet, quiet.
If we are quiet,
if we speak only in whispers,
maybe the Nazis
will not remember we are here.

XIII

Action!
Monday, October 3, 1938

Hast Du zur Arbeit gerade Mut,
Geh' schnell daran, so wird sie gut,
Fällt Dir was ein, so schreib es auf,
Ist heiß das Eisen, hämmre drauf!

Dieses schrieb Dir

Ellen Berger.

d. 3.10.38.

If you have a task to do,
it is best to act fast — delay not!
When you have a thought, write it down.
Strike while the iron is hot!

Yours,
Ellen Berger
October 3, 1938

"Enough," says Father.
"Now is the time!"
And so he has bought
tickets for passage on a ship
that will take us away,
away to America.

It has a lovely name —
the *Aquitania* —
and it is so lovely,
so special,
that it is known as
"The Ship Beautiful."
Father has purchased
tourist-class tickets,
which means, he tells me,
beautiful rooms
(called *cabins* on ships),
one for him and Mother,
another for Ruth and me.
"We will travel in style," he says.
"If we can't take our money with us,
we will spend it on the journey."
Father makes it sound
like a big adventure.
Mother is beginning to pack
bed linens and dishes,
shipping boxes now
so we will have something
old in a new land.

Yet at night I hear
my parents whispering,
because there is still
this one little problem:
We have tickets on a ship beautiful,
but we have no American visas—
and without them,
that ship will sail
without us.

XIV

Not Only in Name
Friday, October 7, 1938

Hamburg, den 7.10.38.

Jüdin nennst Du Dich,
doch nicht nur der Name allein
sondern Herz und Gefühl
müssen auch jüdisch sein.

Dies schrieb Dir zum
Andenken
Friedl Lipka
aus Berlin.

October 7, 1938
You call yourself Jewish,
but not only in name;
heart and feeling
must be Jewish the same.
This was written for you
with thoughts from
Friedl Lipka from Berlin

Jewish, Jewish, Jewish!
I never thought it would matter
so much.
Okay, I am Jewish.
Now can we move on to something else?

But no, it seems Jewishness
has become everything to everybody.
Friedl writes that I must be
more than simply Jewish in name,
but my name is not even Jewish at all:
Jutta Lieselotte.
It's a fine German name.
It's too German for the Nazis,
who also seem to want me to be more Jewish.
They have a new rule that says,
starting next year,
any Jewish girl with a German-sounding name
must add *Sarah* to it
(*Israel* for boys),
so everyone will know
who is Jewish
and who is not.

Not good enough for Friedl!
My heart and sentiments
must be Jewish, too, she writes.
What does this mean?
I should not eat ham, I know,
and I should not tempt Ruth Carlebach with ham.

I should do acts of loving-kindness.
Do I?
I will help Mother with the packing,
and be loving about it.
I will let my sister play with my friends and me,
and be kind to her,
even though she sometimes acts
like a baby.
Is that better?

It is confusing,
thinking about how to be Jewish.
Friedl is an older girl
visiting us from Berlin
with her sister and her parents.
I barely know her,
yet see how she seems to know me.
I am happy when Friedl moves on to a new topic,
which is of great interest to me:
a girl's period,
and what she must do and use and wear
to remain clean and fresh during that time of month.
As I have not yet gotten my period,
I have many questions about this,
and Friedl answers them all.

I will be the most prepared girl ever,
if not the most Jewish.

XV

Trust
Friday, October 7, 1938

Berlin, den 7. 10. 1938.

Vertraue keinem der Dir schmeichelt,
Denn süße Red', ist süßes Gift,
Vertraue dem, der ungeheuchelt
Frei Deines Lebens Schrenken trifft.

Dies schrieb Dir
zum Andenken
Elli Lipka
aus Berlin

Berlin, October 7, 1938
Trust no one who flatters you,
because sweet talk is sweet poison.
Trust only those who honestly
recognize your limits.
This was written for you
with thoughts from
Elli Lipka
from Berlin

How these Lipka girls
look into my heart!
I don't know Elli any better
than I know her older sister, Friedl,
and yet she, too,
cuts close to the bone.

My limits:
I am not so great a student in Hebrew,
a class we must take in our school.
I am not so great in penmanship.
I am not good at piano,
even though I am the daughter of a pianist.
I am a picky eater.

And more to the point:
Yes, Elli, I have a weakness
for sweet talk,
for flattery —
I like them both.
Are they poison?
I know for a fact
it was sweetness and flattery
that got our exit papers
from the Nazis last month.
Father buttered them up
with such sweet talk, plus,
of course,
with a bunch of money and boxes of our pretty
crystal things.

If only the Americans could be sweetened this way—

If sweet talk and flattery could get us our visas, then I really wouldn't care what Elli Lipka thought about it.

XVI

To Poland
Wednesday, October 19,
to Thursday, October 20, 1938

For my dear niece,
with thoughts from Uncle Ludwig
Pabianice, October 19, 1938*

---

* Pabianice is pronounced pub-YAH-nitz or pub-yah-NITZ-a.

October 19, 1938
"Work is not misfortune.
The only concern is the ground
over which a human being works,
and . . . consequences."

*from the writings of Eliza Orzeszkowa** *

To my beloved cousin,
Rita

---

* Eliza Orzeszkowa was a famous Polish writer who lived from 1842 to 1910.

Mother insists
we must visit Poland
one more time
before we sail to America.

And by *we* she means
herself, me, and Ruth,
but not Father,
who must stay home and work,
and by *work*
I think by now
you know what I mean:
It's all about getting those American visas.

Father says no.
It's too dangerous to go to Poland.
Perhaps they won't
let us back into Germany,
perhaps they will snatch us
off the train,
put us in a concentration camp.

Mother doesn't care about *perhaps*.
She cares about Pabianice,
the little city where her parents live,
and Father's mother,
and uncles and aunts and cousins.
She cares about not seeing them
ever again
once we go to America,

an ocean away,
for who can imagine traveling that far
more than once,
even after this Nazi craziness is over.

Father says no.
But Mother insists,
and that is that.

We travel by train,
on a trip we have taken before —
every summer we go to Poland,
every summer we stay
with my Kleinert grandparents,
Marcus and Salka,
and also with Grandma Salzberg.

My grandma Salzberg
lives in a simple house,
without even an indoor toilet,
but she makes Friday night Shabbos
like none other,
with chicken soup and fish and challah
and warmth.

I can walk from Grandma Salzberg
to my Kleinert grandparents,
an easy and shady walk,
pleasant except for the part
where I pass the chicken market.

The chickens wait
for the housewives to choose them.
A chicken that is chosen
gets killed, of course,
and goes to the chicken flicker,
who plucks its feathers
and singes off the ones he can't pluck.
I hold my breath against the nasty burning smell
of the singeing that greets and follows me
on my walk.
And from this comes delicious soup!

My grandpa Marcus,
the dentist,
lets me sit in his laboratory
and see what it is like
to make people new teeth.
He talks about science,
such as the importance of good hygiene
and how we must always wash
the fruit we buy at the market
so we don't get sick from germs.

At both houses,
the feather beds are like
sleeping on clouds,
and everywhere there is family.

There is my aunt Flora,
who is Mother's sister

(and who is a dentist like Grandpa Marcus),
and my cousin Rita,
who is Aunt Flora's daughter,
and Uncle Ludwig,
who is Aunt Flora's husband,
(but who is not Rita's father,
as he is Aunt Flora's second husband),
and there is Aunt Henia,
who is Father's sister
(and whose husband died,
so she lives with Grandma Salzberg),
and cousin Manja,
who is Aunt Henia's daughter.

We have taken this trip many times before,
but never like this,
never with German police searching us —
our bags and our bodies —
on the train.
And we have stayed with our family before,
but never for (maybe) the last time,
which makes things different.
Hugs last longer.
Talk among the grown-ups
is more serious,
and yet some things are the same. . . .

Uncle Ludwig is still the best uncle
(not counting Uncle Max, now in America).
He takes me to his silk factory

and writes his name for me
in the shape of a swan.
Aunt Henia is still the funniest aunt,
who makes me laugh and laugh.
My cousin Rita still likes to walk
all over me when we are sharing the bed
at my Kleinert grandparents' house;
and cousin Manja is still
sweet Manja.

On the train back to Hamburg,
I am tired, and sad,
but also happy,
because visiting Pabianice always makes me happy.
Then we are in the station in Hamburg,
and there is Father,
and he is happy,
because no one snatched us off the train,
no one put us in a concentration camp.
We are together again.

Forward! Over there, to the sun.
Darkness is our eternal enemy,
Over there is bright light.
Over there is truth.
Over there is God.

To my beloved cousin Jutta,
Manja Stahl
Pabianice, October 20, 1938

Have a heart!
Look into a heart!

Pabianice,
October 20, 1938
Manja

XVII

Say Little
Saturday, October 29, 1938

Hear much, say little.
Do not complain to everyone.
Steadfast in misfortune and in fortune,
these are true masterpieces.

To remember,
and all the best for the future,
Your friend,
Ellen Riesenfeld
October 29, 1938

I hear a lot, and so does Ellen.
Too much.
Everyone is talking
about yesterday,
Friday,
when German police burst into homes
before the sun even rose in the sky,
looking for Jews,
specifically, Jews from Poland,
here in Hamburg and everywhere in Germany,
taking them to police stations,
marching them to railroad stations,
putting them on trucks,
sending them away.

I hear so much,
but say little.
I do not say aloud
what I think inside,
which is
why, why,
with my Polish father
and my Polish mother,
was my family not roused before dawn?

But I will heed Ellen's advice,
and I will not speak of this.
I will not complain
of the fear in my stomach,
so cold and sharp.

I will try to remain steadfast
in misfortune and good fortune —
but it is hard,
so hard,
when I hear the footsteps
of the Nazi police
on the marble staircase
going to someone else's apartment,
click-clack-click-clack
click-clack-click-clack.

Click-clack-tick-tock —
as the clock ticks,
and the boots clack,
Father works.
He has traded our tickets
on the beautiful ship *Aquitania,*
for tickets on another ship,
the *Queen Mary,*
which sails much sooner,
in just two weeks,
out of Cherbourg,
in France.

I hear much — oh, too much! —
but also too little.
Where will we be in two weeks?
On a boat with a royal name?
On a truck filled with unwanted Jews?

XVIII

Give Joy Away
Friday, November 4, 1938

Willst Du glücklich sein im Leben
trage bei zu anderen Glück
denn die Freude die wir geben
kehrt ins eigne Herz zurück

Zur freudl. Erinnerung
an
Friedel Schlesinger

Bbg. d. 4. XI. 38

To be happy in life,
spread your joy far and wide.
To give joy away
brings pleasure inside.

In friendship,
Friedel Schlesinger
November 4, 1938

We pack for our journey,
but we can't take everything.
I can take *this* dress,
but not *that* one;
this doll, not the other.
There's no room
for my baby doll carriage,
which I have certainly outgrown,
anyway.
Haven't I?

I know things can be replaced.
But Lilly, my blue parakeet,
who lives in the living room,
she cannot be replaced!
How I'll miss her —
you might be surprised to learn
what a good friend a bird can be.
Frau Krug says she will give Lilly a home,
and take good care of her.

We have visitors from the Nazi police.
They come to inspect our baggage,
to make sure they approve of what we are taking.
They touch our clothing,
folded neatly in the suitcases,
dresses, trousers, nightgowns,
socks, even underwear.
No hidden money?
No.

No jewels tucked away?
No.
They touch and prod,
and when they are satisfied
that we are not depriving the Fatherland
of anything valuable,
they close the suitcases
and seal them shut,
wrapping metal bands around.
I stop watching,
but I smell the heat
of the sealing compound
that fixes the bands around the cases.
We can't put any more in.
We can't take anything out.
If I decide that I packed *that* blouse,
but prefer *this* one,
too bad.

I know
things are not supposed to be important.
I know
things are not supposed to make you happy.
But my things have always brought me joy.
Will leaving them behind —
giving joy away
(to whom? Who will get my roller skates?) —
bring me happiness?
Friedel's poem says it will.
I wonder
what Friedel will have to give away.

XIX

Help!
Friday, November 4, 1938

Edel sei der Mensch,

hilfreich und gut

Zur freundlichen

Erinnerung

Adi Schlesinger

Hmbg. d. 4. 11. 38

Noble is man,
Helpful and good*

In friendly remembrance,
Adi Schlesinger
November 4, 1938

* This quotation is from the writings of Johann Wolfgang von Goethe.

We have train tickets
to get from Germany to France.
We have ship tickets
to get from France to America.
What we don't have—
still—
can you guess?

Father tells us all we must
dress in our good clothes,
whatever has not been packed and sealed,
and come downtown with him—
me, Mother, and Ruth.

We take the streetcar
and soon we are at the American consulate,
the building where the visa people work—
only the consulate is closed.

But Father sees the American officials inside,
so he pounds and pounds on the locked door
until someone comes.
He seems to recognize Father,
and lets us in.

We go upstairs,
upstairs, upstairs,
upstairs,
to the man's office.

He is not a mean man,
the American official,
but he looks at some papers
and tells Father,
"Not yet."
Not yet are there visas for us.
"Maybe next week."

And my father, he explodes!
"Not yet? Next week?
Next week the Nazis could arrest us,
make us disappear,
like our neighbors!
There may not be a next week for us!"

And my father
walks over to the window
of the man's office.
Father opens the window.
It's cold outside;
we don't need fresh air.
But this isn't about fresh air.
As Father looks down to the sidewalk,
far below,
below, below
below this nice office,
he tells the surprised American official
that if he must wait longer for visas,
he might as well jump out the window.

"I might as well jump,"
Father tells the man,
"because the Nazis will be
murdering me soon anyway."

The American official looks at us.
Is he noble, helpful, and good?
No, Vati, don't jump!

XX

Stop, and Go
Sunday, November 6, 1938

Never stop halfway!

With thoughts from
Ilse Stern
November 6, 1938

Good luck!

I am glad that
Father did not follow
my friend Ilse's advice.
He stopped.
I am glad he stopped halfway,
one foot on the windowsill,
when the American official said,
"Mr. Salzberg!"

and gave us visas.

So now it is Sunday,
the day before
we are to leave.
Ilse lives one floor beneath us,
and we have known each other
a long time.
She is not my best friend,
but she is my good friend,
and we see each other
every day.
We will miss each other.
Soon, her family will leave, too,
once they get their visas.
Maybe in America
her family will live downstairs from us
in a new apartment building,
and I'll still see her
every day.

XXI

Until the End
Monday, November 7, 1938

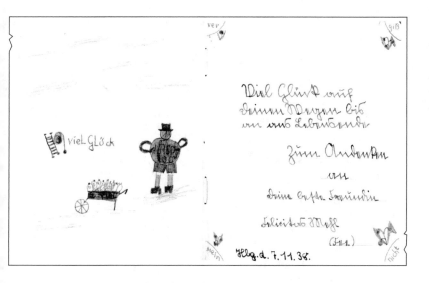

Good luck in all your endeavors
until the end of your life.

With thoughts from your best friend,
Felicitas Mehl
November 7, 1938

We leave tonight
on a midnight train.
It is hard to say
goodbye.
One more goodbye
in this year of goodbyes.
Felicitas and I have played
for many hours.
Now we know
we may never see each other again.
What is there to say?

So good luck, good luck,
here is Mr. Chimney Sweep,
who brings good luck,
with his top hat and his broom
and his ladder,
and the delicate blue blossoms
of forget-me-nots,
as if I could ever forget
my friend Felicitas.
And here is a wheelbarrow
full of fortune,
more good luck.

But the wheelbarrow makes me think
of the *click-clack-click-clack*
that I heard on the stairs last night.
Click-clack-click-clack
click-clack-click-clack —

boots importantly hurrying,
then stopping
one floor beneath ours.

And this morning the Sterns were gone,
Ilse and her parents and brother,
who lived one floor beneath ours.
The Nazi police stopped,
filled their wheelbarrow with the unlucky Sterns,
and clattered off.

XXII

We Waved Until We Couldn't
Monday, November 7, 1938

> November 7. 38.
>
> Heute ist der letzte Tag den ich
> in Hamburg verbringen soll.
> Denn heute fahre ich schon. Ich
> stand sehr früh auf um die
> letzten Sachen und Andenken
> einzupacken. Die Zeit verging
> sehr schnell und es war
> mittag da kam Felizitas
> um sich zu verabschieden.
> Sie schrieb in mein Poesie
> album ein und wir unter=
> hielten uns köstlich. Dann
> verabschiedet sie sich so
> kurz und schmerzlich und
> das war auch vorbei. Eine
> Stunde später kam Herr

Today is the last day that I will be spending in Hamburg, because today we are leaving already. I got up very early to pack the last things and mementos. The time went by very quickly. At midday, my friend Felicitas came to say goodbye. She wrote in my poesiealbum *and we had a very tender conversation. We said farewell to each other, briefly and painfully; then that, too, was over.*

An hour later, Herr Baum came. He didn't know what to say when he saw our empty home. Then Mother and Father came home and the Perlinskys came and we ate supper at Fraulein Katerabich's house. We exchanged gifts. So the time went and the departure was upon us. The Perlinskys cried an awful lot, and Frau Krug also.

We went with the car to the railroad station, and at 12:00 midnight the train came. We waved until we couldn't see anyone anymore.

     —diary entry for November 7, 1938

XXIII

The Train
Tuesday, November 8, 1938

Dann fuhren wir mit
dem Auto nach dem
Bahnhof und um 12 Uhr
kam der Zug. Wir wink-
ten, bis wir nicht mehr
erblicken konnten. Die
nacht verging sehr
schnell und wir waren
in Köln. Wir hatten
eine Stunde zeit und
wir sahen uns Köln
an. Dann ging es weiter
bis nach Paris. In den
Grenzen hatten wir
keine Schwierigkeiten.
dann waren wir über
die Deutsche Grenze.

*The night went by very quickly, and we were in
Cologne. We had one hour of time, and we went
to look at Cologne. Then we continued until we
arrived in Paris. On the border we had no trouble.*
—diary entry for November 8, 1938

I am lying to my diary.
I don't know why,
except maybe some things are too scary
to write down,
even in a diary.
Truth:
This night is endless, not quick.
The border is a tangle of trouble.

From Hamburg to Cologne to Aachen,
still in Germany,
there are Nazi guards on the cars,
carrying rifles with sharp bayonets.
Are we so valuable
they want to guard us?
Not all the passengers
are Jews leaving Germany,
but I think most are.
We sit quietly,
Ruth sleeping,
as the train clatters
away from the lives we know.

In Aachen,
the last town in Germany,
just before we cross into Belgium,
the train stops.
The engine quiets.
A Nazi guard
takes Father off.

We crowd the window,
looking, looking —
we see Father talking,
moving his hands,
reaching into his pockets,
showing his papers,
his small billfold
with a pittance of money.
We can't hear anything.

More Nazis soldiers
join Father and his guard,
more silent talking.
The train engine rumbles to life again;
a whistle sounds.
Soon we will be moving!
Moving without Father!
Vati, say the magic words,
tell them what they want,
give them anything!
Another whistle.

We see Father hand over his billfold.
Now he's walking fast, fast,
to the train.
Now he's back on board!
It all took ten minutes.

What did they want,
the soldiers?

Maybe money,
but Father had only a little.
He was following the law,
and the Nazi law
said we could not take
much money with us.

Soon we are in Belgium.
Another train stop.
Don't take Father again!
I get my wish.
I get better than my wish:
The Nazi soldiers leave the train,
and a few Belgian guards get on.
Our nightmare over,
I can finally sleep.
I wake in Paris, France.

No more lying to you, diary.

XXIV

Paris
Wednesday, November 9
to Friday, November 11, 1938

At the railroad station in Paris was Uncle Romek. In Paris I met a cousin by the name of Guy. He seemed to be very much in love with me, and I felt the same. He looks like Freddie Bartholomew.

—diary entry for November 9–11, 1938

In Paris we have relatives—
my uncle Romek,
who is Mother's brother,
and cousins,
including Guy* Gotthelf,
who looks like the movie star
Freddie Bartholomew,
from *Captains Courageous,*
the last movie I saw at the Waterloo.
How nice he is to me!
—that is, Guy, not Freddie Bartholomew.
His father, Cousin Samuel,
is a real artist.

We visit his art studio,
we visit their home.
It is almost
like a vacation.
When Guy draws a picture for me
in my *poesiealbum,*
I see that he is an artist, too.
One day, I am sure,
Guy will be famous,
either an artist
or a movie star.

*Guy is pronounced *Gee,* with a hard *g,* as in the word *game.*

XXV

Like a Bird
Friday, November 11, 1938

I.

Comme un oiseau dans le ciel noir,
Vous fuyez des vertes plaines
Laissant derrière vous les peines
Et le sillon du désespoir.
Dans ta fuite du temps
        Et des hommes
Serez-vous un jour contents
        Bonhommes?..

Guy Gottbeff
Paris:
128, Avenue
Parmentier

Le 11 Novembre
1938.

Like a bird in the dark sky,
you flee the green plains
leaving behind the pains
and the path of despair.
In the passage of time, and of people,
will you be content one day, my friends?

Guy Gotthelf
Paris
November 11, 1938

The grown-ups can't stop talking
about the news.
Four days ago,
the day we boarded
our midnight train,
a Polish Jewish boy
here in Paris,
Herschel Grynszpan,*
shot and killed
a German government official
who worked at the German embassy in Paris.
Herschel was upset because his parents,
Polish Jews living in Germany,
just like us,
were grabbed from their home
by the Nazis—
this was back in October,
when I heard the *click-clack*
of the Nazis' boots every day—
and were shipped to the border
between Germany and Poland,
with thousands of other *Ostjuden.*
They are sitting there still.
In the cold.

Not welcomed by Poland,
thrown away by Germany.

After Herschel killed the German official,
mobs of Germans back in Germany

* Grynszpan is pronounced GREEN-span.

attacked Jewish homes, businesses, synagogues —
and, of course, Jewish people.
The attacks started
just when we arrived in Paris.
They've continued up to this very moment.
There are fires and broken windows.
Our big synagogue,
where we used to go to services
(but not very often),
has been burned.
Jews are being arrested.
Jews are being killed.
If we had gone to the synagogue more,
if we had prayed more,
if all the Jews had prayed more,
would all of this not be happening?

How lucky we are,
the grown-ups keep saying,
that we left Hamburg
Monday night.
How lucky because of the angry mobs,
but also because Tuesday morning,
before dawn,
at six o'clock,
Nazi police came to our apartment
for us.
We know this because
Father telephoned Frau Krug,
and she told him.

We escaped the Nazis
by six hours.
We are safe.
But my sweet bird, Lilly,
is not safe.
She is dead,
killed by the Nazis,
who were angry that they did not find us at home,
angry that they could not arrest my father
for the crime of being a Jew from Poland,
angry that they could not send us
to the border with Poland
to sit in the cold
with Herschel Grynszpan's parents.

We are like the bird
in Guy's poem—
a bird who has fled a place
of green plains—
our beautiful Hamburg—
and a place
of pains and despair—
ugly Hamburg.
Will we be content one day?
Good question.

XXVI

The Ship
Saturday, November 12
to Thursday, November 17, 1938

> ... nach ... dem Hafen
> Cherbourg. Wir fuhren
> erst mit einer Fähre
> bis zur Queen Mary.
> weil es sehr weit
> draußen lag. Es war
> ein Riesenschiff. Wir
> stiegen auf. Und
> gingen auf das
> Schiff wir in unsere
> Kabine. Wir hatten
> zwei Kabinen
> eine für die Eltern
> und eine für
> uns.

> 13.11.38.
> Sonntag auf dem Schiff Seekrank.
> 14.11.38. Seekrank.
> 15.11.38. Morgens Seekrank. Nach
> mittags auf Deck um im
> Kino
> 16.11.38. Ganzen Tag gut im
> Kino ungebadet
> 17. Ankunft in N.Y.
> Um 6 Uhr sahen wir das
> ganze Meer mit lichtern
> und dann es war ein
> wunderbarer Anblick.
> Als wir vom Schiff herunter
> stiegen waren keine Verwandte
> sie schienen uns vergessen

November 12, 1938. We spent four days in Paris. Then we took our leave from the relatives and boarded a train to the seaport of Cherbourg. There we had to be taken by ferry out to the Queen Mary, *because it was very far out at sea. It was a gigantic ship. We went on the ship and to our cabins. We have two cabins, one for our parents, one for us.*

November 13, 1938. Sunday on the ship, seasick.
November 14, 1938. Seasick.
November 15, 1938. Seasick in the morning.
In the afternoon on the deck and in the movies.
November 16, 1938. Whole day good and
spent at the movies.
November 17, 1938. Arrival in U.S.A. At six
o'clock this morning we saw the whole ocean lit up.
—diary entries

The ship is very big,
and it rolls in the ocean swells.
November is not the best weather
for sailing across the Atlantic Ocean.
So sick, so sick—
but then, suddenly,
not sick,
and they have a nice
movie theater on the *Queen Mary.*
And a heated swimming pool—
for Jews and non-Jews.

Mother wakes me Thursday morning
to see the ocean on fire—
only there is no flame, no fire;
it is the harbor of New York City
ablaze with the lights of ships,
and it is the tall lady,
the Statue of Liberty,

holding her torch
and watching over us,
everyone from the *Queen Mary*
crowding together on the deck
to stare up at her.

Dockworkers move about on the piers —
their skin is brown, even black,
such as I have never seen before.
Giant buildings loom beyond the harbor —
these are the skyscrapers I have heard of,
taller than anything we have at home.

We are here in America.
This will be my home now.
No Nazi soldiers, but also no friends.
I am starting my new life.
Who will write in my *poesiealbum*?

Afterword

As Jutta stood at the rail of the *Queen Mary* on that November morning in 1938, gaping at the lights and sights of New York City, she could not imagine what her new life in the United States would be like. Nor could Jutta imagine the fate of many of her friends and relatives who had written in her *poesiealbum.* Nor did she yet really understand what she and her family had escaped.

Jutta Salzberg, my mother, was born in 1926 in Hamburg, Germany. Her younger sister, my aunt Ruth, was born in 1930. Their parents, Isaac Salzberg and Rose Kleinert, were both originally from the town of Pabianice, in Poland, near the city of Lodz. In Hamburg, Rose and Isaac were neither rich nor poor, but comfortably in the middle. Though Jewish, Isaac and Rose were not strict in their religious practices. Isaac and Rose spoke Polish and German, but barely spoke Yiddish, the popular language of European Jews. Although

they had many friends and a busy social life —
dinner parties, theatergoing, playing cards —
they were not prominent in the German-Jewish
community, and not political.

But beginning in 1933, whether the Salzbergs
were religious or not, important or not, rich or not,
political or not, did not matter. In that year, Adolf
Hitler came to power in Germany. Hitler and
his political party, the Nazi Party (for National
Socialist Party) made hatred of Jews the official
policy of Germany. Anyone who was a member
of what the Nazis called the Jewish "race" was
considered less than fully human. Nazi Germany
began systematically to cut Jews out of German
life. Hitler's goal was to create a nation that was
Judenrein — without Jews.

The Nuremberg Laws in 1935 stripped
Jews in Germany of their political rights and also
banned marriage between Germans and Jews.
Other decrees forbade or limited Jews from
working in many types of professions and
businesses. My grandfather Isaac began the
process of emigrating to the United States shortly
after these laws were enacted. But things moved
slowly with the American immigration officials.
The U.S. immigration laws put limits — called
quotas — on how many people could come to the
United States, and where they could come from.
Other countries had similar immigration systems
that severely limited how many Jews from

Germany could enter their lands. Isaac waited for the officials at the United States consulate in Hamburg to tell him they had visas for him and his family to go to the United States. He waited throughout 1936. He waited throughout 1937. And then it was 1938, the year of my mother's *poesiealbum.*

The year 1938 was a critical one for Jews in Germany, particularly for so-called *Ostjuden* — Jews such as my grandparents Isaac and Rose, who came from nations to the east of Germany, mainly Poland. Although the Nazis had not yet devised their policy of exterminating the Jews in Germany and Austria (and later, Jews in other European countries the Nazis took over), they did decide in 1938 that *Ostjuden* should be expelled from Germany and Austria. If these Jews did not find ways to leave Germany and Austria, they were to be rounded up and held in concentration camps. Still other Jews were targeted for arrest and detention in concentration camps because of their real or supposed political activities.

Unfortunately, although the United States and other free countries were aware of the dire situation faced by Jews in Nazi Germany and Austria, these nations refused to increase their immigration quotas. Thousands upon thousands of Jews who wanted to flee the Nazis could not, because countries such as the United States failed to open their doors to them. In the summer of 1938, representatives from thirty-two nations held a conference in Evian, France, to address the worsening problem of Jewish refugees. (Refugees are people who are forced to leave their homes in search of other countries to live.) The representatives all agreed that the situation for Jews living under Nazi rule was grave. But, one by one, the representatives also offered reasons why their countries would not be expanding their immigration quotas to let more Jewish people in.

Throughout 1938, Jews in Germany grew desperate to leave the country. More and more turned to suicide—choosing a quick death rather than whatever fate the Nazis had in store for them. So when Isaac Salzberg—my grandfather—put his foot on the sill of the window in the consulate's office that November morning, his action must have seemed completely believable to the American official who witnessed it. The Americans in Germany knew how despairing the Jews had become.

Such was the atmosphere in which my mother and her friends lived. They were not aware of the exact dimensions of the Nazi threat—no one was. Communications in those days were neither instant nor always reliable. But by listening to their parents talk and by sharing stories with each other, they learned that their world was dangerous, tense, and subject to disruption at any minute.

And yet—my mother and her friends found ways to do things that were at least a little normal. They fooled around and gossiped during recess at school, even though they had to be quiet so as not to disturb the school's neighbors. They had birthday parties. They exercised at the Jewish Bar Kochba Gymnastics Club. And they wrote in each other's *poesiealbums.*

My mother, aunt, and grandparents were incredibly fortunate. They were fortunate on Friday, October 28, 1938, when Nazi police raided homes throughout Germany—including Hamburg—arresting *Ostjuden* by the thousands and sending them by truck and train toward the Polish border. The Polish government refused to allow most of these people to enter their country. The result was chaos and misery at the German-Polish border, with Jews stranded in railroad stations, sleeping in open fields, and crowded into camps. Seventeen-year-old Herschel Grynszpan, a Jewish boy living in Paris, got a postcard from his sister describing how she and their parents had been expelled from their home in Hanover, Germany, as part of the late October action and were stuck on the border. He sought revenge by shooting Ernst vom Rath, a German official working at the German embassy in Paris. Grynszpan's action, in turn, helped spur a surge of violence against the Jews remaining in Germany—sometimes called *Kristallnacht,* or Night of Broken Glass, and also known as the November

Pogrom—which my mother and her family heard about once they arrived in Paris.

Why did the Nazis overlook my mother's family on October 28, 1938? It is impossible to know for certain. But one reason may be that my grandfather Isaac, although from Poland, did not have proper Polish papers proving him to be a Polish citizen. This made him, in essence, stateless— a man without a country. Being stateless is not normally a useful thing. But in this case it might have saved his life, and that of his family. Because my grandfather Isaac did not have a proper Polish passport (a passport is a travel document from one's country of citizenship), he was not registered with the German police as a Polish citizen—and so they may not have had him on their list of Jews to grab on October 28.

Some of my mother's friends and their families also escaped being arrested, expelled, or murdered by the Nazis. Others were not so lucky. They were imprisoned or killed as part of the Nazis' grisly campaign against Jews—later called the Holocaust—which continued until May 1945, when Nazi Germany was finally defeated in World War II.

Some of the information about what happened to my mother's friends and family comes from personal interviews with survivors. In other cases, especially with regard to people who perished in the Holocaust, I have obtained records of their fate from Yad Vashem, the Holocaust memorial and museum in Jerusalem, Israel. Yad Vashem has collected a vast amount of information about victims of the Nazis and published this compilation as The Central Database of Shoah Victims' Names. (*Shoah* is the Hebrew word for the Holocaust.) I have also used the substantial research facilities of the United States Holocaust Museum in Washington, D.C.

Here is what happened to the people of my mother's *poesiealbum.*

HANNELORE ASCHER (CHAPTER XII). In July 1942, the Nazis transported Hannelore to Auschwitz, a large concentration camp complex they created in Poland. She was sixteen years old. Auschwitz included three separate camps, including one dedicated to the mass murder of Jews and other people. Hannelore died at the hands of the Nazis in Auschwitz.

ILSE BEHREND (later Ilse Wesel) (CHAPTER X). Ilse came to the United States from Nazi Germany, escaping the Holocaust. She settled in New York.

ELLEN BERGER (CHAPTER XIII). Ellen died at the hands of the Nazis in Auschwitz in 1943.

RUTH CARLEBACH (CHAPTER IV). In December 1941, when Ruth was fifteen years old, the Nazis transported her to Riga, Latvia, which by then was in German hands

The Nazis created a ghetto in Riga and concentration camps nearby; they also used the Rumbula Forest, outside the city, as a mass killing site. Only a tiny fraction of Jews sent from Germany to Riga survived. Ruth died in Riga at the hands of the Nazis.

ELLEN DAVIDSOHN (CHAPTER IX) came to the United States from Nazi Germany, escaping the Holocaust.

GUY GOTTHELF (CHAPTERS XXIV–XXV). My mother found her Parisian cousin Guy so good-looking and so talented that she predicted he would be famous. Guy did achieve fame, although not the kind my mom hoped for. After Nazi Germany conquered France in June 1940, Guy joined the French Resistance—people who continued fighting for freedom against the Nazis. On August 25, 1944, Guy was killed while on a mission for the French Resistance near Paris. He was twenty-one years old. The Resistance leaders of the town of Yerres, the suburb of Paris where Guy lived, named a street after him in honor of his sacrifice. Rue Guy Gotthelf still exists today in Yerres. Guy's father, the artist Samuel Gotthelf, was also killed by the Nazis.

REBEKKA HERMANNSEN (CHAPTER VIII). In October 1941, the Nazis transported Rebekka to the Lodz Ghetto. She was fourteen years old. Lodz was a city in central Poland where the Nazis created a large, crowded Jewish ghetto after

Germany conquered Poland in September 1939. Many people in the Lodz Ghetto died of starvation and disease. Other residents were transported from Lodz to Auschwitz or the Chelmno extermination camp, and systematically murdered there. Rebekka died at the hands of the Nazis in the Lodz Ghetto.

ILSE HESS (later Ilse Bechhofer)(CHAPTER III). Ilse came to the United States in 1940. After World War II, she moved back to Germany with her husband and their children.

FLORA KERNER AND RITA LEWIN (later Flora Adin and Rita Hilton)(CHAPTER XVI). My mother's cousin Rita and Rita's mother, Flora, were forced by the Nazis into the Lodz Ghetto. (The city of Pabianice, where my mother's Polish relatives lived, was only a few miles from the larger city of Lodz. Most Jewish residents of Pabianice were forced into the Lodz Ghetto after the Nazis took over Poland.) Rita and Flora survived the Lodz Ghetto and were transported by the Nazis to Auschwitz. From there, the Nazis sent Rita and Flora to another concentration camp, Bergen-Belsen. They survived Bergen-Belsen and came to the United States after World War II. Today Rita lives in Florida.

UNCLE LUDWIG (Ludwig Kerner) (CHAPTER XVI). After the Nazis took over Poland in September 1939, German soldiers arrested Uncle Ludwig. His family never saw him again.

GRANDMA SALKA KLEINERT AND GRANDPA MARCUS KLEINERT (CHAPTER XVI). Grandpa Kleinert died at the hands of the Nazis in the Lodz Ghetto. Grandma Salka Kleinert survived the Lodz Ghetto but was taken by the Nazis to Auschwitz, where she was killed by the Nazis.

FELICITAS MEHL (later Felicity Rose) (CHAPTER XXI). Felicitas escaped Nazi Germany by going to England with the *Kindertransport.* Today she lives in Nottingham, England. The *Kindertransport,* or Children's Transport, was a program organized by citizens of Great Britain after they heard of the terrible *Kristallnacht* attacks on Jews in Germany in November 1938. The program allowed children (but not their parents) to travel from Nazi Germany to Great Britain, where they lived with foster families, in orphanages, or worked on farms. The *Kindertransport* ran from December 1938 to September 1939, and allowed nearly 10,000 children to escape Nazi Germany.

ELLEN RIESENFELD (CHAPTER XVII). In November 1941, the Nazis transported Ellen to Minsk, which was a city in the German-occupied Soviet Union. The Nazis killed many of the Jews they sent to Minsk immediately upon their arrival. Those who were not immediately killed were crowded into a ghetto and pressed into slave labor for the Nazi war effort. Ellen died in Minsk at the hands of the Nazis.

EVA ROSENBAUM (later Eva Abraham-Podietz)

(CHAPTER VII). Eva went to England with the *Kindertransport* in December 1938. After World War II, Eva lived in England, Israel, and Brazil. In 1959, she came to the United States. Today she lives in Philadelphia.

UNCLE MAX AND AUNT ALICE (CHAPTER III). Max and Alice Salzberg immigrated to the United States in 1936. They lived in Detroit, Michigan, where Uncle Max worked in the jewelry business. Despite their hopes, they never did have a child.

GRANDMA REBECCA SALZBERG (CHAPTER XVI). The Nazis first forced Grandma Salzberg into the Lodz Ghetto, and later to Auschwitz, where they killed her.

ADI SCHLESINGER (later Adi Fulda) (CHAPTER XIX). Adi remained in Germany until May 1940, when her family escaped to Italy, and from there to the United States. She and her family settled in New York City, where she lives today.

FRIEDEL SCHLESINGER (CHAPTER XVIII). In December 1941, the Nazis transported Friedel (who was Adi Schlesinger's cousin) to Riga. She was fourteen years old. Friedel died in Riga at the hands of the Nazis.

MANJA AND HENIA STAHL (CHAPTER XVI). My mother's cousin Manja and her mother, Henia, were forced by the Nazis into the Lodz Ghetto, and later to concentration camps. The Nazis killed Henia at Auschwitz. They killed Manja at

Stutthof concentration camp.

LISA STREIT (later Lisa Kohlman) (CHAPTER II). Lisa and her family came to the United States early in 1938. Many years later, when both Lisa and my mother were more than seventy years old, they discovered that they lived five miles apart in the Maryland suburbs of Washington, D.C. Lisa lives in Maryland today.

INGE WEISS (CHAPTER IV). In November 1941, when Inge was fifteen years old, the Nazis transported her to Minsk. Inge died in Minsk at the hands of the Nazis.

I have been unable to trace Elli Lipka, Friedl Lipka, Ruth Sperber, Cilly Seligmann, and Ilse Stern. As they are not listed in any of the compilations of names, or eyewitness accounts, of Holocaust victims that I consulted, I can only hope that they escaped Nazi Germany and moved on to enjoy long and happy lives.

As for my mother and her family, they split up almost as soon as they arrived in New York. Isaac Salzberg's two brothers, who lived in Detroit, urged him to come to that Midwestern city. However, to ease the burden on the family, my mother was sent to live with a childless aunt and uncle in Washington, D.C. They only spoke Yiddish; my mother only spoke German. She was desperately lonely. After several months of separation, the family reunited in New York City. There they rented a tiny tenement infested with bedbugs and visited by the occasional rat. My grandfather earned money by selling buttons and ribbons door to door.

My mother went to a public elementary school in New York, near the family's apartment building. Because she could not speak English, the teacher sat her in the back of the classroom. Mom did not make many friends during the several months that she attended this school. Her closest schoolmate, May Corbitt, was also forced by the teacher to sit in the back of the room. This was not because May was Jewish or foreign—it was because she was African American.

Some of my mother's classmates in her New York City school wrote in her *poesiealbum* in June of 1939. For example:

The teacher is a good old soul,
She goes to church on Sunday.
She prays to God to give her strength
To kill us kids on Monday.

Or:

I love I love I love you so well:
If I had a peanut I'd give you the shell.

Clearly, as my mother found, American girls had different standards for their autograph albums than she and her friends back in Germany had for their *poesiealbums*.

By the fall of 1939, my mother and her family had relocated once again—and together—to Washington, D.C. My mother's father changed his name from Isaac to Edward. He thought it sounded more American. For a while, the adults in her life urged my mother to change her name, too. They tried Yetta, Henrietta, Julia—anything but *Jutta*, which Americans seemed unable to pronounce. JUH-tah. JEW-tah.

My mother resisted. Enough had been taken. She kept her name: Jutta. When she met my father—Harold Levy, an American serviceman whose medical treatment of wounded men while under German attack earned him the Legion of Merit medal during World War II—he had no problem at all pronouncing it. In 1952 they married, and my mother became Jutta Levy. They lived in Maryland and had two children: myself and my sister, Sharon. My mother's sister, Ruth Horwitz, also settled in Maryland with her husband and had two children.

In 1998, my mother heard that one of her Hamburg classmates from the Jewish School for Girls was living in Chicago, Illinois, the city where my husband's parents lived. Not only did this classmate, Irene Bettink (now Irene Biro), live in Chicago—she lived across the street from my husband's parents. My mother promptly invited

Irene and her husband to visit Washington, D.C. A few months later the two old friends were hugging in front of my parents' home.

"As we were saying . . ." Irene began.

". . . before we were so rudely interrupted," my mother completed the sentence.

They continued their conversation as if exactly sixty years had not passed since the last time they spoke.

Around the same time, I wrote an article for *The Washington Post* about my mother and her family's departure from Hamburg on that midnight train. Two more of the girls—now women, of course—who attended school with my mother in Hamburg and who immigrated to the United States, saw it. They called one another to ask: "Is this"—the Jutta I wrote about in my article— "*our* Jutta?" (You can be sure that they said YU-tah.) After concluding that my mother was their Jutta, one of them—Lotte Heilbrunn (now Lotte Blaustein)—wrote a letter to me saying, "I immediately dug out my old Poesie Album and re-inspected the class picture. Sure enough, we're all there way back in 1938 at the old school. . . ."

Two years later, in 2000, seven of the "girls" from the Jewish School for Girls in Hamburg reunited in Washington, D.C. Besides my mother (now Jutta Levy), they included two people who wrote in my mother's *poesiealbum*—Lisa Streit (now Lisa Kohlman) and Eva Rosenbaum (now

Eva Abraham-Podietz). The other classmates were Irene Bettink (now Irene Biro), Lotte Heilbrunn (now Lotte Blaustein), Gerda Irene Seckel (now Irene Rehbock), and Celia Horwitz (now Celia Lee). Celia traveled the farthest to reach the gathering, flying in from England.

The women brought photographs, letters, documents, and articles to their little reunion. They brought *poesiealbums*. They sang snippets of songs they remembered from their school days in Hamburg. For three days straight, these seven women talked and laughed and cried together as if they had known each other their whole lives — which, in a way, they had.

JUTTA'S PHOTOS

Jutta and her sister, Ruth

Jutta in her beret

Jutta after swimming

Jutta in the park

Rose and Isaac, Jutta's parents

Inside Jutta's Hamburg apartment

Family picnic in Hamburg

Jutta's German travel document

Logo for Samuel Gotthelf's studio

Jutta on board the Queen Mary

Jutta, at age 18, in Washington, D.C.

Time Line

1926

Jutta is born in Hamburg, Germany.

1933

The Nazi Party, let by Adolf Hitler, takes power in Germany. The new government adopts anti-Jewish laws and creates the first concentration camp, Dachau, near the city of Munich. One of the earliest anti-Jewish measures is the Law Against the Overcrowding of German Schools, which aims to exclude Jews from public schools.

1934

Jutta leaves public school to enroll in the Jewish School for Girls.

1935

The German government enacts the Nuremberg Laws. These laws and others adopted in subsequent years exclude Jews from virtually all aspects of the nation's life.

1936

Germany hosts the Olympic Games. While in the international spotlight, the Nazi government softens some of its anti-Jewish pronouncements.

1937

Jutta's father, Isaac Salzberg, is forced to shut down his business because he is Jewish.

1938

March: German troops enter neighboring Austria. The country becomes a part of Germany in a takeover known as the *Anschluss*. Austria's Jews are immediately subject to anti-Jewish laws, as well as to degrading treatment and street violence.

June: Nazi police conduct mass arrests of Jews throughout Germany. Many of those arrested are imprisoned in Buchenwald concentration camp, near the city of Weimar.

July: Representatives of thirty-two nations gather in the resort town of Evian, France, to discuss the problem of Jewish refugees seeking to flee Nazi persecution. The Evian Conference produces no tangible results, as the nations decline to loosen the immigration restrictions that prevent the refugees from entering their countries.

October 28: Nazi police raid homes throughout Germany, rounding up thousands of *Ostjuden* (Jews from east), particulary Jews from Poland, and sending them to the German-Polish border.

Class photo

Jutta's report card

A homemade
New Year's card

Train to Poland

Aunt Alice   *Uncle Max*

Grandpa Marcus the dentist

Grandma Salzberg

Grandparents Kleinert

Aunt Henia

Vacationing near Pabianice

Jutta with cousin Man
in Pabianice

Dessert in Pabianice

November 7: *Jutta and her family leave Germany on a midnight train. They arrive in Paris, France the following morning.*

In Paris, Herschel Grynszpan, a Jewish teenager from Hanover, Germany, assassinates Ernst vom Rath, a German official.

November 9–10: German citizens attack Jewish shops, Jewish people, and synagogues throughout Germany. The attackers are spurred on by news of the vom Rath assassination. The event becomes known as *Kristallnacht* (Night of Broken Glass), or the November Pogrom. Similar attacks and destruction occur in Austria.

November 12: *Jutta and her family depart France on board the* Queen Mary, *a British ocean liner.*

On the French-German border, hundreds of Jews attempting to flee Germany are turned back by French officials.

November 17: *Jutta and her family arrive in New York.*

1939
Germany invades Poland on September 1. World War II begins.

A Note on Sources

The research for this book began with Jutta Levy's oral history and her personal documentary materials, but it did not end there. The historical events that Jutta recalled in her interviews — from the appearance of anti-Jewish signs in Hamburg storefronts to the *Queen Mary*'s arrival in New York harbor on November 17, 1938 — were confirmed and, if necessary, corrected by reference to a variety of other sources and materials. These included interviews and memoirs of other individuals; news articles from the time period; records of government and nongovernment agencies; academic articles; and books.

This research frequently took me, as research will, in unanticipated directions. For example, a simple Google search on the name of my mother's French cousin, Guy Gotthelf, yielded — to my great surprise — a digital map of "Rue Guy Gotthelf" in the town of Yerres, France. I made contacts in Paris who followed up by unearthing handwritten records from the World War II–era archives of a committee of the French Resistance. The records, dated September and December 1944, indicated that Guy was a member of the Resistance who died that year at the age of twenty-one on a mission against France's Nazi occupiers. The records further reflected the committee's decision to honor Guy by naming a street in Yerres after him. And so Jutta's brief encounter with her cousin in 1938, when she was twelve and he fifteen, as Europe's turmoil propelled them into their vastly dissimilar futures, took on a deeper meaning than I could have imagined.

What follows is a selection of the sources consulted in researching *The Year of Goodbyes*.

Selected Bibliography

Adler, David. *We Remember the Holocaust*. New York: Holt, 1989.

American Jewish Committee. *American Jewish Yearbooks*. Philadelphia: American Jewish Committee, 1933–1939. www.ajcarchives.org.

Benjamin and Vladka Meed Registry of Holocaust Survivors. United States Holocaust Memorial Museum, 100 Raoul Wallenberg Place, S.W., Washington, D.C.

The Central Database of Shoah Victims' Names. Yad Vashem: The Martyrs' and Heroes' Remembrance Authority Web site. www.yadvashem.org.

Dawidowicz, Lucy S. *The War Against the Jews, 1933-1945*. New York: Holt, 1975.

Fox, Anne L., and Eva Abraham-Podietz. *Ten Thousand Children: True Stories Told by Children Who Escaped the Holocaust on the Kindertransport*. West Orange, N.J.: Behrman House, 1999.

Friedländer, Saul. *Nazi Germany and the Jews, Volume 1: The Years of Persecution, 1933-1939*. New York: HarperCollins, 1997.

Hamburger jüdische Opfer des Nationalsozialismus: *Gedenkbuch* [Memorial Book for Hamburg Jewish Victims of the Nazis]. 1995 ed. Staatsarchiv Hamburg.

Holocaust Encyclopedia. United States Holocaust Memorial Museum Web site. Numerous articles, time lines, maps, and photographs. www.ushmm. org/wlc/en.

Kaplan, Marion A. *Between Dignity and Despair: Jewish Life in Nazi Germany*. New York: Oxford University Press, 1998.

Mosel, Wilhelm. "No. 35 Karolinenstrasse (Israelitische Töchterschule)." *Wegweiser zu den ehemaligen Staetten jüdischen Lebens oder Leidens in den Stadtteilen Neustadt, St. Pauli* [Guide to the former sites of Jewish life or suffering in the districts of Neustadt, St. Pauli]. Hamburg: Deutsch-Jüdische Gesellschaft, 1983. www1. uni-hamburg.de/rz3a035//karolinenstrasse1.html.

Wilhelm Mosel wrote and published this and many other detailed booklets about the fate of Hamburg's Jewish community under the Nazi regime. They are of limited availability in libraries, but have been made available on a University of Hamburg Web site and translated by Struan Robertson for *A History of Jews in Hamburg*, www1.uni-hamburg.de/rz3a035/ jh_welcome.html.

New York Times. Numerous articles from 1938 reporting on developments relating to Germany and Austria.

Nicholas, Lynn H. *Cruel World: The Children of Europe in the Nazi Web*. New York: Knopf, 2005.

Schuman, Frederick L. *Europe on the Eve: The Crisis of Diplomacy, 1933-1939*. New York: Knopf, 1942.

Shirer, William L. *Berlin Diary: The Journal of a Foreign Correspondent, 1934-1941*. New York: Knopf, 1941.

United States Holocaust Memorial Museum. *Historical Atlas of the Holocaust*. New York: Macmillan, 1996.

Zapruder, Alexandra. *Salvaged Pages: Young Writers' Diaries of the Holocaust*. New Haven, Conn: Yale University Press, 2002.

Acknowledgments

I hardly have words to thank my mother, Jutta Levy, for her efforts in helping me shape her story into this book.

I am grateful to Eva Abraham-Podietz, Ingrid Bastien, Gilles Baumont, Gary Alan Bechhofer, Julian Berengaut, Irene Biro, Lotte Blaustein, Adi Fulda, Jean-Marc Grosfort, Rita Hilton, Ruth Horwitz, Lisa Kohlman, Celia Lee, Stephanie Owens Lurie, Irene Rehbock, Felicity Rose, and Brendan Ross.

Loving thanks to my husband, Rick Hoffman, for encouraging this project and for much helpful feedback on the manuscript.

I would like to acknowledge the people of my mother's *poesiealbum* whom I have been unable to find. I would like to honor those who did not survive.

Wer Dich liebt hat als ich,
der schreibe sich noch hinter mich.

Zum Andenken
an Deine Schwester
❀ Ruth ❀

Das Datum weiß ich
leider nicht, ich glaub es heißt
Vergißmeinnicht.

*Whoever loves you more than me
should write behind me, certainly.* *
With thoughts from your sister,
Ruth
The date is something I forgot,
I think it's called
Forget-Me-Not. **

* This is a poem that children often wrote on the final page of a
poesiealbum. The joke was, as there were no more pages to write on, no one could
possibly write "behind" this last poem—and therefore, no one could love
the *poesiealbum*'s owner more than the writer. In this case, the writer was
Jutta's sister, Ruth.

** And this is another clever *poesiealbum* feature—sometimes girls
didn't write the date, but instead wrote this little verse that played off the
rhyme with the word for the forget-me-not flower.